PART ONE

NINETEEN FOURTEEN

In August 1914 the Central Powers of Europe (Germany and Austria-Hungary) went to war with the Allied Powers (Great Britain, France and Russia). Each country had a carefully prepared plan of war.

Germany's **Schlieffen Plan** was to defeat France in six weeks by invading at high speed through Belgium. Then the German armies could turn to fight the Russians, 1000 kilometres away to the east. France had **Plan Seventeen** – an all-out attack on the provinces of Alsace and Lorraine by soldiers trained to fight hard and fast, whatever the odds against them might be. Great Britain had a small but well trained **Expeditionary Force** ready to cross the English Channel to defend Belgium and France against the Germans. Austria's **Plan R** was to send huge forces across the border into Russia. Russia planned to do the same in reverse.

Each of these plans had been worked out to the last detail. The key to their success was speed. Every army was to be taken to battle in thousands of railway trains and would overwhelm the enemy by sheer force of numbers. The generals in every country were sure that the war they were starting would be over in a matter of months, perhaps even weeks.

However, none of the war plans worked in the way they were meant to and the war was not over in weeks. It lasted for four years and three months – 215 weeks. During that time nearly fifty million men wearing the uniforms of thirty different countries took part in a world-wide war, the first of its kind. By its end, ten million of them had lost their lives and twice that many had been wounded or crippled. At least nine million civilians also lay dead, victims of murder, disease and starvation.

Perhaps the generals who made their careful plans would have thought differently if they had listened to the words of an old German general, Helmuth von Moltke, who once said 'In war there are always three courses of action open to the enemy, and he usually chooses the fourth'.

This book tells the story of how the war plans of every country went wrong because their enemies usually chose the 'fourth course' – the unexpected that nobody had made plans for.

1

1

THE WAR PLANS FAIL IN THE WEST

German soldiers marching towards the River Marne, September 1914

War plans in the west

The Great War began exactly according to plan. A million grey-uniformed Germans were packed into 6480 railway trains at stations all over Germany. The trains began rolling at three-minute intervals towards Belgium. Farther south, three great armies of French soldiers in bright blue tunics gathered on the German border to invade the province of Lorraine. In the English Channel troop ships from Britain nosed their way into French ports and 125,000 khaki-clad men of the British Expeditionary Force (BEF) streamed down the gangways, ready to march east.

It took only three weeks for the war plans to go wrong. When the German 1st and 2nd Armies marched into Belgium they met tougher fighting than expected. The Belgian army fought bravely and slowed them down for ten days in a battle at Liège. Then the British Expeditionary Force, which the Germans called 'a contemptible little army', slowed down the 1st Army in a battle at **Mons**. The British rifle-fire at Mons was so fast and accurate that the Germans thought they were being machine-gunned. For the rest of the war the BEF was proud to be called 'The Old Contemptibles'.

While the Germans were being slowed down in Belgium, the French were being torn to pieces in Lorraine. Their orders were to attack with '*élan*' (speed) and '*cran*' (guts) but they found themselves charging at well-defended machine-gun posts. Speed and guts were useless against these and 300,000 French soldiers were mown down in just two weeks. Plan Seventeen had failed completely.

Now Germany's invasion of France went wrong. Far away in the east, the Russian army attacked Germany sooner than expected so von Moltke, the German commander, sent part of his armies to fight them. This meant he had fewer men for the attack on France. Next, the 1st Army, led by General von

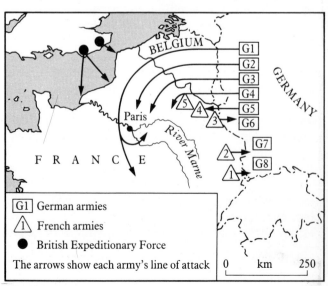

The line-up of the armies

2

Kluck, ran into difficulties. As you can see from the map on the opposite page, Kluck's army (G1) had the farthest to go. His men often had to march 50 kilometres a day under a blazing hot sun, and they were exhausted by the time they reached France. Finally, the Germans found they were under attack from an unexpected direction, for now that Plan Seventeen had failed, the French were marching back from Lorraine to cut the Germans off.

The Battle of the Marne

Despite these setbacks the Germans pressed forward until they reached the River Marne. By 4 September some were so close to Paris that they could see the Eiffel Tower in the distance. For a while it seemed that the Schlieffen Plan would work. But then Moltke and the German generals made a fatal mistake. Instead of going west to surround Paris as planned, Kluck's army went east of Paris towards the Marne. It was this that gave the French a chance to save themselves.

As you can see from the map below, the French armies were marching west to cut the Germans off. To help them, the Military Governor of Paris, Marshal Galliéni, rounded up 250 taxis from the streets of the city and used them to send reserve soldiers to the Marne. Day and night, starting on 4 September, the 'taxis of the Marne' shuttled back and forth taking fresh troops to fight the exhausted Germans.

The **Battle of the Marne** lasted a week (5–11 September) and was one of the biggest ever fought. Two million men battled along a 240 kilometre front around the river. Gradually the French and the BEF drove the Germans back. By the end of the week they had retreated 60 kilometres to the River Aisne where they dug trenches and set up machine-gun posts to defend themselves.

The race to the sea

The Battle of the Marne saved the French for the time being and the rival generals now wondered what to do. Abandoning their original war plans they each tried to outflank the other – that is to get round the side of an army to cut it off. The French, the BEF and the Germans all set off north, hoping to outflank each other before they reached the English Channel. During this 'race to the sea', terrible battles were fought, the worst of them at **Ypres**. There the BEF stopped the Germans from outflanking them, but at an appalling cost. One British division lost 365 of its 400 officers and 10,774 of its 12,000 soldiers.

Neither side won the race to the sea so they started to dig trenches to stop the other from advancing. Gradually the lines of trenches lengthened so that by the end of 1914 they stretched all the way from Flanders in Belgium to Switzerland in the south. The armies could no longer move. It was stalemate.

The Battle of the Marne

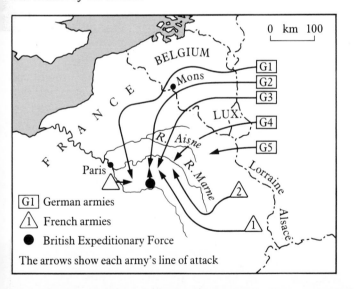

The 'race to the sea'

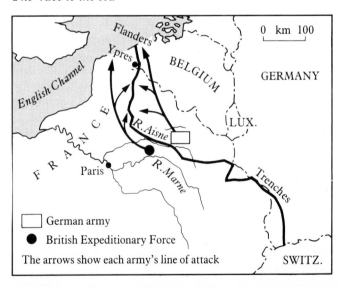

Work section

Study these newspaper headlines of 4 September and 8 September 1914. Then answer these questions.

1. How did Paris 'throw up new defenses' on the day this paper appeared? Who was in charge of the new defences?
2. In what ways did the German armies seem to be in a strong position on 4 September?
3. Explain in detail the second headline, 'Germans pushed back . . .'.

3

THE WAR PLANS FAIL IN THE EAST

War plans in the east

Just as the Schlieffen Plan had failed in the western part of Europe, so the war plans in the east also failed.

As you know, the Germans aimed to defeat France in six weeks so that they could send the bulk of their armies to fight the Russians in the east. When Schlieffen made this plan, he thought that Germany would be safe for those six weeks because the Russian army was slow and poorly trained, and would not be able to start moving quickly.

But Schlieffen was wrong. The Russians took only ten days to get four of their armies on the march, two heading for Germany and two for Austria-Hungary.

On 19 August the Russian 1st Army smashed into Germany and won a battle at Gumbinnen. On the same day, General Samsonov led the Russian 2nd Army into German territory. You can see from the map opposite that these two armies were closing around the Masurian Lakes, aiming to squeeze the Germans between them.

At first the Russians were successful. The Germans retreated in panic. Newspapers in France and Britain rushed out headlines praising 'the Russian Steam Roller' and predicted that it would soon be rolling into Berlin. Rumours spread throughout Britain that the Russians had landed in Scotland and were marching south to join the British Expeditionary Force. Countless stories were told of fur-hatted Russians marching south with snow still on their boots. Some were even seen trying to fit roubles (Russian coins) into slot machines in London!

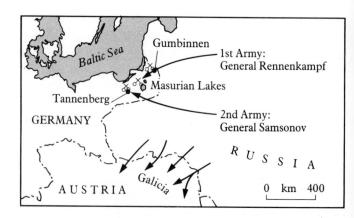

Defeat for the Russians

In reality, the Russian steam roller had already started to break down. The German general in the east was sacked and two experienced generals, Hindenburg and Ludendorff, were sent to take his place. When they arrived at the scene of the fighting they saw that the two Russian armies were cut off from each other by the Masurian Lakes, a huge area of marsh and forest. Ludendorff immediately took advantage of this weakness and massed the German army for an attack on Samsonov's 2nd Army near the town of Tannenberg.

Fighting began on 25 August and for the next five days there was terrible slaughter. A German politician, General von Moltke, tells us in his memoirs what happened:

'The horrors of it are so ghastly that an

Russian troops crossing a river during the Battle of Tannenberg, August 1914

eye-witness, an officer who has just returned, says it will live in his dreams until his dying day. The sight of thousands of Russians driven into two huge lakes or swamps to drown was ghastly, and the cries and shrieks of the dying men and horses he will never forget. So fearful was the sight of these thousands of men, with their guns, horses and ammunition struggling in the water, that, to shorten their agony, they turned the machine-guns on them. But even in spite of that there was movement seen among them for a week after. And the mowing down of the cavalry brigade, 500 men on white horses, all killed and packed so closely that they remained standing. The officer says this was the ghastliest sight of the whole war.'

After five days of fighting at the **Battle of Tannenberg** the Russians had lost 125,000 men and the Germans 13,000. General Samsonov, defeated and disgraced, disappeared into the forest and shot himself.

Now the Germans were loaded into railway trains and rushed to the north of the lakes to fight the Russian 1st Army. They were joined by reinforcements arriving from France. On 5 September they attacked and another awful slaughter took place.

The Russians retreated in mad panic, many to drown in the marshes, the lucky ones to their own country. In this **Battle of the Masurian Lakes** a further 100,000 Russians died. In all a quarter of a million Russians had been killed in the space of a month.

Victory for the Russians

Farther south it was a different story, for the Russians were victorious against the armies of Austria-Hungary. Following Plan R, the Austrians made a massive attack across the Russian border. They quickly captured great areas of land and their flag flew over countless towns and villages. But within a week they ran into five Russian armies and were stopped in their tracks. As heavy autumn rain began to fall, the Austrians turned and fled. Thousands deserted, leaving heavy guns and ammunition behind them. In four days the Austrians retreated over 200 kilometres.

This was a tremendous victory for Russia. They had captured the entire province of Galicia and were now in a position to attack Germany from the south. Moreover, the Austrians were also being beaten in their attack on Serbia (see map on page 6). Already a quarter of a million Austrians had died in the fighting.

Work section

A. Read this account by the French Ambassador to Russia of a meeting he had with Tsar Nicholas of Russia in December 1914. Then answer the questions beneath.

> 'The Tsar lit his cigarette, offered me a light, and went straight to the heart of the subject: "Great things have happened in the three months since I saw you last. The splendid French army and my dear army have already given such proofs of valour [*bravery*] that victory can't fail us now".'

1. Make a list of the events that you think Nicholas had in mind when he said 'Great things have happened in the three months since I saw you last'.
2. Do you agree with Nicholas that the French army and his own army had shown such bravery that they were bound to win the war? Explain your answer.

B. Study this British cartoon of September 1914 and answer the following questions:
1. Name the Austrian emperor who is running away from the steam roller. Which part of Austria-Hungary is he running away from?
2. Why do you think the cartoonist has pictured Russia as a steam roller? In your opinion, was it accurate to compare Russia with a steam roller? Explain both your answers.

C. 1. If you had been in Britain in 1914 why would you have refused to believe the rumours that Russians were marching 'with snow on their boots' to join the BEF?
2. Why do you think millions of British people did believe such rumours?

D. Study the photograph on the opposite page. Do you think it was taken before or after the battle of Tannenberg? Give reasons for your answer.

THE WAR SPREADS

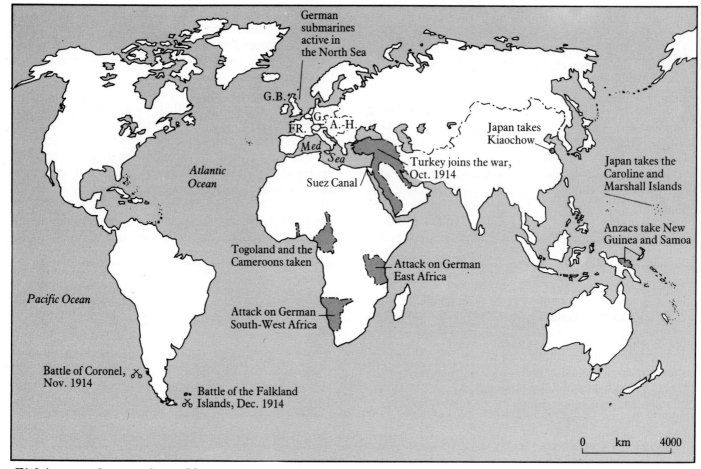

Fighting spreads across the world

The Great War began as a war between European countries but it took only three weeks to spread to other parts of the world.

Japan and Turkey join the war

Japan was the first non-European country to join the fighting. Japan had made an alliance with Britain in 1902 and now helped her by attacking Germany's colonies in the Far East. Japanese armies quickly captured Kiaochow and then the Caroline and Marshall Islands in the Pacific Ocean.

The next non-European power to join was Turkey. Enver Bey, the Turkish ruler, was not at first sure whether to side with Britain or with Germany. Both countries had been trying to win his friendship by helping to improve the Turkish armed forces. Britain, for example, was building two of the most modern super-Dreadnought battleships for the Turkish navy. The British and the Germans both wanted Enver Bey's friendship because Turkey could give them valuable help in the war. Turkey could be especially useful to

Germany by attacking Russia from the south and by seizing the Suez Canal, Britain's vital trading link with her colonies in the Far east.

Enver Bey finally decided to join Germany because three days before the war began, the British decided not to give the new ships they were building to Turkey. Enver Bey was furious. When the Germans offered him two of their own warships, the *Goeben* and the *Breslau*, as replacements, he leapt at the gift.

Britain, however, was determined not to let the Turks have the German ships, and sent eleven warships to capture them. There followed a dramatic chase at top speed through the Mediterranean Sea. In the boiler rooms of the *Goeben*, stokers shovelled coal frantically into the furnaces. Four died in the scorching heat and dozens dropped from exhaustion. But the German ships kept up their speed and gave the British ships the slip. After a week of racing they arrived safely in Turkish waters. With this gift now in his hands, Enver Bey had no choice but to join the war against Russia, France and Britain (October 1914).

War at sea

The British Royal Navy was involved in sea battles in other parts of the world in 1914. In the Pacific Ocean, a German squadron of five ships led by Admiral von Spee came upon a smaller squadron of British ships near **Coronel** on the coast of Chile. The British ships were old and slow, and von Spee found them at dusk, silhouetted against the sunset. It took him only an hour to sink them.

To deal with von Spee's dangerous squadron, the British government sent seven warships to the south Atlantic with orders not to return until they had sunk it. While the British ships were refuelling in the **Falkland Islands**, Admiral von Spee's squadron arrived to attack the Falklands' radio station, not realising that the Royal Navy was there. The British immediately gave chase and sank four out of the five ships. Two thousand three hundred German sailors were drowned, including von Spee and his sons.

Closer to home, there were no great battles at sea. Before 1914, the naval planners had put all their efforts into making big ships with big guns – the Dreadnoughts. Few of them foresaw that submarines could be as deadly as battleships. On 22 September three British warships were sunk by a single German submarine, or **U-boat**. In November the British Grand Fleet fled from the North Sea when they saw a U-boat periscope. Although this was in fact a false alarm, the Grand Fleet did not return to the North Sea until 1915. This meant that German warships were free to attack the British coast. People in Bridlington and West Hartlepool were killed when German warships bombarded them with shell-fire.

War in the colonies

Elsewhere in the world there was small-scale fighting in Germany's colonies. Togoland in Africa was captured and an attack started on the Cameroons. In November, the Allies attacked German East Africa while, in the Pacific, Australians and New Zealanders (known as Anzacs) took the German colonies in New Guinea and Samoa. Anzacs also went to the Persian Gulf to capture the oil wells there, while the South Africans conquered German South West Africa.

Men from Britain's Empire were drawn into the fighting because they were, in theory, subjects of King George V. So not only did they fight in the overseas states but in Europe as well. Both Canada and India sent powerful armies to fight in France. The war which had begun in Europe was rapidly becoming a world-wide war.

Work section

A. This British poster aimed to persuade men from Britain's Empire to volunteer for the fighting.
1. What is the 'Old Lion' meant to be and what were the 'Young Lions'?
2. The poster is headed 'The Empire Needs Men'. Why was it important for Britain to get the help of the overseas states in her empire?
3. If you had been a Canadian or Australian in 1914, would this poster have made you want to volunteer for the fighting? Explain your answer.

B. Make notes on *The Events of 1914* before going any farther. You could copy out the revision guide on the next page or, if you prefer, use it as a plan for notes of your own. Whatever method of note-making you decide to use, draw or trace maps from pages 1–6 to illustrate your notes.

THE EMPIRE NEEDS MEN!

THE OVERSEAS STATES

All answer the call.

Helped by the YOUNG LIONS
The OLD LION defies his Foes.

ENLIST NOW.

Revision guide: the events of 1914

A. Events on the Western Front

1. Five German armies invaded Belgium and then France in August 1914. They aimed to defeat France in six weeks before going east to fight the Russians.

2. The German invasion did not go according to plan because
   a) the Belgians fought bravely and slowed down the German advance;
   b) the British Expeditionary Force slowed the Germans again at the **Battle of Mons**;
   c) the French armies, after being beaten in their attack on Lorraine, marched west to cut off the German advance.

3. The German invasion of France was halted at the **Battle of the Marne** (September 1914):
   a) The German commander, Moltke, ordered the 1st Army to go east of Paris instead of west. This allowed the French and the BEF to concentrate their forces along the River Marne. They were reinforced by reserve soldiers sent by taxi from Paris by General Galliéni.
   b) After a week of heavy fighting the Germans retreated to the River Aisne where they dug trenches to protect themselves.

4. Both sides then started a 'race to the sea', trying to outflank each other. After fierce fighting, especially at the **Battle of Ypres** (October–November 1914), a stalemate developed because neither side could outflank the other.

5. Both sides then started to dig trenches to stop each other from advancing. The line of trenches quickly lengthened until it stretched 760 kilometres from Flanders in Belgium to Switzerland.

B. Events on the Eastern Front

1. The Russian armies mobilised more quickly than the Germans thought possible. The 'Russian steam-roller' invaded Germany on 19 August and won minor victories.

2. Two new generals, **Hindenburg** and **Ludendorff**, were sent to deal with the Russian invasion, and were given reinforcements from the Western Front. They beat the Russians in major battles at **Tannenberg** and the **Masurian Lakes**. Russia lost 250,000 men.

3. Russia also invaded Austria-Hungary. This was more successful. They captured the province of **Galicia**, making it possible to attack Germany from the south.

C. The spread of the war

1. **Japan** joined the fighting on Britain's side and took Kiaochow and some Pacific Islands from Germany.

2. **Turkey** joined on Germany's side after being given the German warships **Goeben** and **Breslau**.

3. Fighting at sea took place at **Coronel** and the **Falkland Islands**. No sea battles took place in the North Sea because of the threat of **German U-boats**.

4. **Men from Britain's Empire**, especially Australia, New Zealand, India, Canada and South Africa, fought in Africa and the Middle East as well as on the Western Front in Europe.

Test your understanding of the events of 1914

'We can be at Paris within a fortnight. You will be home before the leaves have fallen'
  (Kaiser Wilhelm speaking to German soldiers in August 1914)

'The war will be over by Christmas'
  (a popular saying in Britain in 1914)

Write a short essay explaining:
a) what these quotations mean;
b) why so many people thought like this in 1914; and
c) why these statements turned out to be wrong.

A French cartoon published at the start of 1915.
What point do you think the cartoonist was trying to make?

At the start of 1915, the war which should have been 'over by Christmas' was nowhere near an end. Britain's war leader, Lord Kitchener, said 'I don't know what is to be done. This isn't war'.

The problem was that none of Europe's war leaders knew how to end the stalemate in France. They had made their plans for a quick war between fast-moving armies, but now their armies were at a halt, digging trenches to stop the other side from advancing. They tried using new kinds of powerful weapons and they thought up new methods of attack. But both sides simply strengthened their trenches to deal with these, making the deadlock even harder to break.

On the Allied side, some war leaders thought they knew what was to be done, but there was

disagreement. The generals wanted to pour millions more men into the trenches for an all-out assault on the German lines. Some politicians were not convinced, saying that the war could never be won on the Western Front. They wanted to attack Germany and her allies from a different direction – from Turkey in the east of Europe.

Both the 'westerners' and the 'easterners', as the arguing war leaders were known, had their chance to try out their ideas in 1915. The 'easterners' attacked Gallipoli in Turkey, while the 'westerners' launched massive attacks on the Western Front, hoping to deal Germany a knock-out blow.

Both were proved wrong. As we shall see, 1915 was a year of disasters for the Allies.

4

THE GALLIPOLI CAMPAIGN

Allied troops landing at Anzac Cove in the summer of 1915. The barrels on the beach contain water: all the troops' supplies has to be brought in to them by sea

When Turkey joined the war on Germany's side and became one of the Central Powers, it was a serious blow to the Allies. The Turkish navy closed the **Dardanelles**, the narrow straits linking the Mediterranean with the Black Sea. This cut off the supply of food and arms to Russia just at the time when she most needed them.

Churchill's plan

To help their Russian allies, the British planned a bold invasion of Turkey. Winston Churchill, First Lord of

the Admiralty and one of the 'easterners', said that the Royal Navy could capture the Gallipoli peninsula, north of the Dardanelles. One politician later said that Churchill's plan was 'the only imaginative conception [*idea*] of the war'. The two maps below show just how imaginative it was.

The first map shows the difficult position that the Allies were in at the start of 1915 – stalemate on the Western Front, Russia under attack from all the Central Powers and cut off from supplies by the closure of the Dardanelles.

The second map shows what Churchill aimed to do

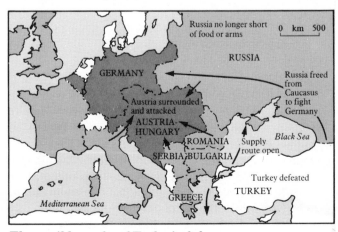

The position of the Allies in early 1915

The possible results of Turkey's defeat

10

by attacking Gallipoli: first to capture the Turkish capital, Constantinople, and so knock Turkey out of the war: second to re-open the supply route to Russia. Churchill also hoped that the defeat of Turkey would have other important effects. The neutral countries close to Turkey – Greece, Romania and Bulgaria – would then join the Allies, allowing them to surround Austria for an all-out attack. Austria's defeat would leave Germany isolated and unable to continue fighting. In short, the Gallipoli campaign would be the beginning of the end of the war.

Attack on Gallipoli

A fleet of British and French ships began the attack on Gallipoli in February 1915. The Turks, however, had put mines in the water and three battleships were blown up when they sailed into the Dardanelles. The rest of the fleet rapidly retreated.

Although Winston Churchill claimed that the whole operation could be carried out by the Navy, the Allies now decided to send an army to Gallipoli. A force of British and Anzac troops was gathered together and put under the command of Sir Ian Hamilton. None of them had ever practised landing on an enemy coast before and Sir Ian Hamilton was sent to Turkey without proper maps for planning his invasion. He was also very slow in making his preparations when he got there.

When the Anzacs finally landed in **Anzac Cove** on 25 April the Turks were ready for them. Thousands were mown down by machine-gun fire as they left their landing craft. Those who made it through the blood-stained sea were pinned down on the beaches by shell-fire from the cliffs above.

The Allies attacked again in August at **Suvla Bay** but this attack was as disastrous as the first. The historian, A.J.P. Taylor, has written about it in these words:

'20,000 men were put ashore almost without loss; only a thousand Turks, without machine guns, barred their way. Here Stopford was in command. He did not go ashore. Instead he congratulated the men on their successful landing and settled down for his afternoon nap. On shore

the men were told to relax; they went off to bathe, with no Turks between them and victory.'

When the order to advance was given two days later, the Turks had brought up reinforcements and halted the attackers. Both sides dug trenches and, as on the Western Front, there was stalemate. In their trenches, the Allies were plagued by disease, insects, water shortages and hunger.

In Britain, many people criticised the generals leading the campaign, and Sir Ian Hamilton was sacked. A new commander, Sir Charles Monro, realised that he could never conquer Gallipoli and decided on a complete withdrawal. During the last weeks of 1915 nearly all Allied soldiers were evacuated from Gallipoli. This was the only successful part of the campaign for they escaped without the loss of a single life.

The Gallipoli campaign had cost the Allies 200,000 casualties and the Dardanelles were still closed to Russian ships. Russia now faced the prospect of slow starvation.

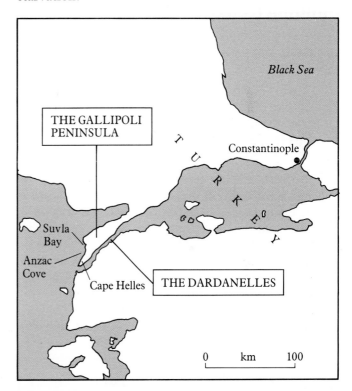

THE GALLIPOLI PENINSULA

Black Sea

Constantinople

Suvla Bay

Anzac Cove

Cape Helles

THE DARDANELLES

TURKEY

GREECE

0   km   100

Work section

A. Study the photograph on the opposite page. Make a list of the difficulties that the Allies seem to be facing in this scene.

B. Compare these two comments on the Gallipoli campaign made by British historians:

'The Gallipoli Campaign of 1915 was the most imaginative. . .and the most important single operation in the whole course of the two world wars'   (Alan Moorehead)

'It was a massive failure, ruining reputations and wasting lives'   (R.R. James)

1. Judging by what you have read, which of these two opinions do you most agree with? Explain your answer.
2. Why do you think historians have such different opinions about the Gallipoli campaign?
3. Re-read A.J.P. Taylor's account of the attack on Suvla Bay. What does his opinion of the Gallipoli campaign seem to be?

5

TRENCH WARFARE

After the failure of the Gallipoli campaign the 'westerner' generals were even more certain that the war could only be won on the Western Front. They pinned their hopes on breaking the stalemate by making massive assaults on the German trench lines. Before reading the story of these assaults, you need to find out about the lives that soldiers on both sides were leading in the trenches, and about the weapons they were using against each other.

Building trenches

Trenches were built wherever the enemy was found, no matter what was in the way. A German soldier wrote:

> 'Part of our trench went through a cemetery. We cleared out the contents of the family vaults and used them to shelter ourselves from artillery fire; hits from heavy shells would hurl the coffins and semi rotted corpses high into the air.'

The diagram and photographs here show how trenches were built. A trench was usually at least 2 metres deep and 2 metres wide, and was dug in a zig-zag so that the blast from an exploding shell would be confined to only a small section of the trench. There were normally three lines of trenches on each side of the 'no-man's land' that divided the enemy armies. In the front line, trenches were built with firing steps and elbow rests to help the soldiers shoot over the top. Behind these were the support trenches and behind those were the reserve trenches.

Connecting the three lines were communication trenches. There were also 'blind alleys' to confuse the enemy in case of a successful attack, and 'saps' which were shallow trenches leading to look-out posts or machine-gun nests.

Life in the trenches

The following accounts show us that for most soldiers life in the trenches was a horrifying experience. What every soldier feared most was 'going over the top'. This meant climbing over the parapet and charging at the enemy trenches in an attempt to capture them. A young German tells us what often happened:

> 'At noon we went over the top. After less than a hundred yards we ran up against an almost concrete wall of whistling and whining machine-gun bullets. My company commander had his face shot away; another man yelling and whimpering held his hands to his belly and, through his fingers, his stomach protruded. A young boy cried for his mother, bright red blood spurting out from his face.'

Before soldiers were sent over the top, the enemy trenches were bombarded with shells from heavy guns to try to kill the front-line troops and to tear gaps in the barbed wire defending them. A British sergeant wrote this about the effects of shelling:

> 'It was on May 2nd that . . . this single high explosive shell killed 7 and wounded 18 – yet the

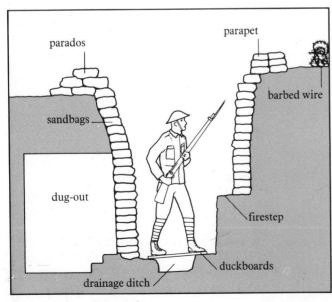

Cross-section of a trench

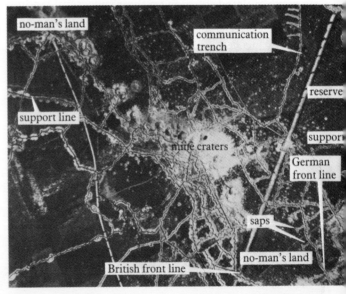

Line of trenches as seen on an aerial photograph taken in France in 1915

A deep, well-built British trench protected by barbed wire. Can you spot the periscope covered with sacking which the sentry is using to watch the German front line?

day before 400 shells came over and dropped behind the trench and no one was hurt. The trench after the dead and wounded were removed presented a ghastly sight – it was red with blood like a room papered in crimson.'

The very noise of shells exploding gave many men 'shell-shock'. This is how a young British soldier from Wiltshire was affected:

'His steel hat was at the back of his head and his mouth slobbered, and two comrades could not hold him still. These badly shell-shocked boys clawed their mouths ceaselessly. Others sat in the field hospitals in a state of coma, dazed as though deaf, and actually dumb.'

When they were not fighting or being bombarded, soldiers in the trenches lived a miserable life. When it rained they often spent days knee-deep in water or mud, and this could lead to 'trench foot':

'Your feet swell up two or three times their normal size and go completely dead. You could stick a bayonet into them and not feel a thing. If you are fortunate enough not to lose your feet and the swelling begins to go down, it is then that the . . . agony begins. I have heard men cry and even scream with the pain and many had to have their feet and legs amputated.'

Then there were the rats and the lice. A pair of rats can produce 880 offspring in a year, and even dry, clean trenches swarmed with them. A British officer wrote:

'There are millions! Some are huge fellows, nearly as big as cats. Several of our men were awakened to find a rat snuggling down under the blanket alongside them.'

Most soldiers got lice because they often had to go without washing or changing their clothes for weeks at a time. For George Coppard, the result was that:

'The things lay in the seams of trousers, in the deep furrows of . . . woolly pants. A lighted candle applied where they were thickest made them pop like Chinese crackers. After a session of this, my face would be covered with small blood spots, from extra big fellows which had popped too vigorously.'

In theory, soldiers in the trenches had plenty to eat. Judge for yourself from this list made by a British soldier in his notebook:

List of army rations: 1 man per diem (day)		
Meat (bully beef)	1 lb	[453g]
Bread (or biscuits)	1¼ lb	[567g]
Bacon	¼ lb	[113g]
Tea	½ oz	[14g]
Sugar	2 oz	[56g]
Jam	2 oz	[56g]
Cheese	1 oz	[28g]
Butter	¾ oz	[21g]
Potatoes	¾ lb	[340g]
Salt	1 oz	[28g]
Pepper	1/36 oz	[0·7g]
Mustard	1/20 oz	[1·4g]

But cooking in the trenches was difficult. A soldier from Hull describes a typical meal of

'. . . bully beef [corned beef] and biscuits, and plum and apple jam and biscuits, washed down with tea flavoured from the previous meal, cooked in the same container as the water was boiled, onion being predominant.'

At the end of his day in the trench, a soldier might be able to get a few hours sleep in his dug-out and, if he was not exhausted, perhaps dream of home and hope that next day he would 'catch a blighty one' – a wound that would not kill or maim him, but serious enough to get him sent back to 'Blighty' – Britain.

Work section

A. Copy or trace the photograph of trenches seen from above. Label your diagram to show all the following kinds of trenches: front-line, support, reserve and communication trenches, blind alleys and 'saps'.

B. Use the evidence in this chapter to write a diary of a soldier's experiences during one week in a front-line trench.

6

NEW WEAPONS

During 1915 the generals on the Western Front used huge numbers of weapons in an attempt to break the stalemate. Some were recent inventions and more deadly than any of the weapons used in previous wars.

Heavy artillery

The weapon which most generals liked best was heavy artillery, the big guns. As you know, both sides bombarded each other with explosive shells before starting an attack. The big guns which fired the shells had enormous power. The new howitzers could fire shells which exploded into metal splinters called shrapnel over a distance of 13 kilometres. Soldiers in the front line could tell what sort of shell was coming by the noise it made in the air. The British, for example, called German 77-millimetre shells 'whizz-bangs'.

The effects of heavy artillery fire were horrifying. As one French gunner reported:

> 'You have no idea of the number of Boches [Germans] blown to bits. What a horrible sight in the woods in which not a single tree has been spared. Human remains, arms or legs, knapsacks, blankets, etc. hung on the spruces. We watched Boches flying up in the air as much as three or four hundred feet.'

The big guns fired huge numbers of shells. In 1915, 400,000 were used every month on the Western Front. The noise made by the constant bombardment was shattering. It damaged men's brains and made their ears bleed, and it also gave them shell-shock. The shells also churned up the land into a sea of muddy

A howitzer gun in action during the Ypres fighting, 1917 (see page 31)

craters that made attacks on the enemy trenches even more difficult.

Machine-guns

At the start of the war many of the Allied generals did not think the machine-gun was an important weapon. To them it was still a recent and untested invention. The Germans, however, could see its usefulness right from the start. A water-cooled machine-gun like the Vickers gun fired 600 bullets a minute. Soldiers on the attack could be mown down in minutes by a hail of lead, as this German machine-gunner reports:

> 'The officers were in front. I noticed one of them walking calmly carrying a walking stick. When we started firing we just had to load and re-load. They went down in their hundreds. You didn't have to aim, we just fired into them.'

A German machine gun crew in 1914

Tanks

One new weapon of 1915 was invented and built in Britain by a designer of farm machinery. It was an armour-plated tractor which moved at 6 kilometres per hour and was armed with both cannons and machine-guns. For security reasons it was code-named 'the tank'. When tanks were first used in battle in 1916, the Germans were so scared by the sight that they panicked and fled. A British rifleman described seeing tanks for the first time:

> 'There before our astonished eyes appeared about six of the first Mark 1 tanks, lurching about the country on their caterpillar tracks . . . bursting through hedges, crossing trenches, demolishing walls and even snapping off small trees.'

A tank crosses the British trench on the way to an attack in 1916

Grenades

For close-range fighting, soldiers were trained to use bayonets – long knives fixed to the ends of their rifles – but it was difficult to use these in attacks on trenches. By 1915 many soldiers preferred to use hand grenades instead. The British used the pineapple-shaped Mills Bomb, while the Germans used stick-shaped grenades known as 'potato mashers'.

Gas

Poison gas was another new weapon used in the Great War. It was first used on 22 April 1915 by German troops at the Second Battle of Ypres. A British officer who was watching from a trench nearby describes the effect of chlorine gas on the French troops:

'Dusk was falling when from the German trenches in front of the French lines rose that strange green cloud of death. . . . In the gathering dark of that awful night they fought with their terror, running blindly in the gas cloud, and dropping with chests heaving in agony and the slow poison of suffocation mantling their dark faces. Hundreds of them fell and died. Others lay helpless, froth upon their agonised lips and their racked bodies powerfully sick, with searing nausea at short intervals. They too would die later – a slow and lingering death of unimaginable agony.'

Chlorine gas worked by suffocating the lungs. So did phosgene gas which was invented soon after. Mustard gas was far worse even than this. Its effects did not show for hours after a gas attack. Then it began to rot the body. The victim's skin blistered and his eyes bulged out. The lining of the lungs was stripped raw. The pain was so great that many victims had to be strapped to their beds.

Fortunately, both sides soon stopped using gas because it was easy to counter its effect with gas masks. In the early days, soldiers breathed through cotton pads soaked either in chemicals or in their own urine. Later, helmets with breathing masks were introduced and by 1917 every soldier had an effective gas mask.

A soldier prepares to throw a grenade, during the Battle of the Somme. How can you tell he is German?

Work section

A. Test your understanding of this chapter by explaining what all the following words mean: artillery, shells, shrapnel, howitzer, machine-gun, bayonet, grenade, phosgene gas.

B. Use the information in this chapter to give answers to the following question:
1. Why, according to the German machine-gunner, was the machine-gun such an effective weapon?
2. What advantages are suggested by the British rifleman in his account of using tanks on the battlefield?
3. a) Why do you think it was difficult to use bayonets in trench warfare?
   b) Why did soldiers prefer to use grenades for close-range fighting?
   c) Can you think of any disadvantages involved in the use of grenades?
4. Two famous historians have written very different things about the use of poison gas at the Second Battle of Ypres:

'Gas is the least inhumane [*cruel*] of modern weapons.'   (B. Liddell Hart)
'This was not only wicked. It was folly.'   (A.J.P. Taylor)

Which of these opinions do you agree with? Explain your answer.

7

DISASTER ON ALL FRONTS

The remains of a soldier after an attack on the enemy trenches

The Western Front

The 'westerner' generals had no shortage of men to fight the battles they were planning on the Western Front. The French had millions of conscripts (men who are forced to join the army) while the British had over a million volunteers who had been encouraged to join the army by recruiting campaigns. Posters like the one below made many men feel they ought to enlist.

With millions of soldiers at their command, the Allied generals felt sure of victory. The sheer weight of their numbers would be enough to break the German trench lines. Before sending his men into battle at **Neuve Chapelle**, the British commander, Sir Douglas Haig, ordered that 'The attacks are to be pressed regardless of loss'. The attacks failed, however. After three days of fighting the loss was 11,000 men, but only a few square kilometres of land were gained. The French suffered an even greater loss: 50,000 were killed in an attack near **Compiègne** but all they won was 500 metres of land.

Next month, on 22 April 1915, it was the turn of the Germans to attack. At the **Second Battle of Ypres**,

Daddy, what did YOU do in the Great War?

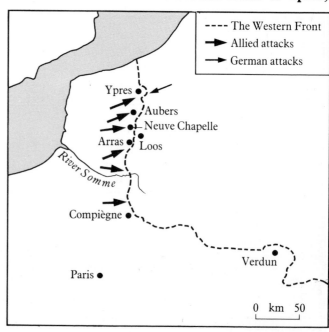

Map legend:
- ----- The Western Front
- → Allied attacks
- → German attacks

Ypres
Aubers
Neuve Chapelle
Arras — Loos
River Somme
Compiègne
Verdun
Paris

0　km　50

French troops looking out from their trenches saw green clouds of chlorine gas drifting towards them. Two whole brigades were 'gassed' before reinforcements arrived to halt the Germans.

In May, the Allied generals tried another advance. The French lost 120,000 men in an attack at **Arras**. At **Aubers**, the British were sent 'over the top' in a solid line. When the German machine-gunners saw an unbroken line of khaki uniforms coming towards them, their officers ordered them to 'fire until the barrels burst'.

By June the Allies had won 10 square kilometres of land from the Germans but had lost 300,000 men. With so many soldiers being killed, the British had to mount new recruiting campaigns to replace them. Many of the young men who stepped forward to fight were sent straight to their deaths. In September, six entire divisions – 108,000 men – went over the top in the terrible **Battle of Loos**, and again the German machine-gunners had a perfect target. After eleven days of slaughter the battle was called off with 60,000 British corpses left lying on the battlefield.

Other Fronts

The Allied generals had even less success on other fighting fronts. In central Europe, the Germans decided to crush Serbia which was still holding out against the Austrian army. King Ferdinand of Bulgaria was tempted by promises of land to join the Central Powers, so Serbia was soon under attack from three countries.

In an attempt to help the Serbs, the Allies sent troops to Salonika in Greece. The opening of the **Salonika Front** was actually a waste of time, for Greece was not at war with the Central Powers. The Allies were therefore able to do very little fighting there.

Meanwhile the Serbs were being crushed. Many thousands tried to escape to the sea by crossing the icy mountains of Albania. During the three weeks they spent in the frozen mountain passes, over 20,000 died of exposure, exhaustion and disease.

Farther north, on the Eastern Front, the Russians were retreating, for the Germans had sent reinforcements to help the Austrian army drive them out of Galicia which they had captured in 1914. By the end of 1915 the Russians had fled nearly 300 kilometres back into their own country.

One other fighting front was opened in 1915 – the **Isonzo Front** in Italy. Italy joined the war on the side of the Allies when they promised to give her land and money at the end of the war.

Italian soldiers began fighting in May but without much success. They were badly trained, badly led, and their equipment was poor. They also had to fight in appalling conditions, for the border with Austria was a high mountain range. They advanced slowly along icy cliffs and through glaciers, uphill all the way until they reached the Isonzo river. There they had to fight eleven battles just to get across the Austrian border. They suffered huge losses of men but only gained 10 kilometres of ground. Yet another fighting front had turned to stalemate.

New areas of fighting in 1915

Work section

A. This is an account by Winston Churchill of a meeting he had in 1915 with Lord Kitchener, Britain's Minister of War. Read it and then answer the questions below.

'He looked at me sideways with a very odd expression on his face. . . . He told me that he had agreed with the French to a great offensive in France. I said at once that there was no chance of success. He said that the scale [*size*] would restore everything. . . . He had an air of suppressed excitement like a man who has taken a decision of terrible uncertainty.'

1. a) Name one of the great offensives in France that Lord Kitchener agreed to make in 1915.
   b) What was the result of this offensive?
2. a) Why do you think that Winston Churchill said that there was no chance of success?
   b) What action did he want to take instead of an offensive on the Western Front?
3. Can you suggest a reason why Lord Kitchener looked like 'a man who has taken a decision of terrible uncertainty'?

B. Study the recruiting poster on the opposite page. Explain how it was intended to make men want to enlist in the army.

C. Make notes on *The Events of 1915* before going any farther. You could copy out the revision guide on the next page or you could use it as a plan for notes of your own. Illustrate your notes with maps.

Revision guide

A. At the start of 1915 there was a **stalemate on the Western Front**. Politicians and generals disagreed about what to do; the 'easterners' wanted to invade Turkey, the weakest of the Central Powers. The 'westerners' wanted to break through the Western Front with massed attacks on the German trenches.

B. **The Gallipoli Campaign**
1. The aims of the campaign were to
   a) capture the Gallipoli peninsula and defeat Turkey,
   b) open the supply route to Russia through the Dardanelles,
   c) bring neutral countries such as Greece and Rumania onto the Allied side, then
   d) surround Austria for an all-out attack.

2. The campaign began, on Winston Churchill's advice, with a naval attack on Gallipoli but was called off after three warships were sunk by Turkish mines.

3. The campaign was then handed over to the army. British, French and Anzac troops invaded Gallipoli in April but were quickly beaten back by the Turks.

4. A second attack at Suvla Bay also failed. By this time, over 200,000 Allied troops had died in Gallipoli.

5. The campaign was called off in November and all Allied troops were evacuated without loss of life in December – the only successful part of the campaign.

C. **Events on the Western Front**
1. Allied troops made a number of offensives against the German trench lines throughout 1915. The biggest attacks took place in

March	– the Battle of Neuve Chapelle.
April	– the Second Battle of Ypres.
May	– the Battles of Arras and Aubers.
September	– the Battle of Loos.

2. 300,000 Allied soldiers were killed in these battles but very little land was gained from the Germans.

D. **Events on the other fronts**
1. Bulgaria joined the Central Powers and helped them crush Serbia.
2. The Allies tried to help Serbia by sending troops to Salonika in Greece, but this achieved nothing.
3. The Russians were driven out of Galicia and made to retreat 300 kilometres.
4. Italy joined the war on the Allied side but the Italian attack on Austria failed, and stalemate set in on the Isonzo Front.

E. **New Weapons** were used in 1915 in an attempt to break the stalemate. As well as artillery bombardments, the machine-gun, grenades and gas were used. They killed hundreds of thousands of men but did not produce the hoped-for breakthrough.

F. **Trench warfare** was the reason why neither side could break the stalemate. Armies defended themselves by digging deep trenches protected with barbed wire. It was usually impossible to get across the 'no-man's land' that divided the enemy trenches, even when thousands of men attacked together. Both sides therefore had to stay on the defensive in their trenches, mostly in appalling conditions.

For discussion or debate

Who, in your opinion, was right about how to break the stalemate of 1915 – the 'easterners' or the 'westerners'? Begin by making a list of arguments in favour of each point of view, e.g.:

The 'easterners' thought that	The 'westerners' thought that
1. They should attack Turkey because she was the weakest of the Central Powers and easier to defeat than Germany.	1. If they had enough soldiers, they could break through the Western Front and defeat Germany.

Then decide which set of arguments you find most convincing, and explain why.

PART
THREE
NINETEEN SIXTEEN

Some of the 315,000 Frenchmen who died at Verdun

The names of three battles sum up the year 1916 – **Verdun**, the **Somme**, and **Jutland**.

At the start of 1916 the Central Powers were in a stronger position than the Allies. The Germans were still holding the Western Front while the Russians were in headlong retreat in the east. This allowed **General Falkenhayn**, Germany's supreme commander, to bring half a million more men from Russia to fight on the Western Front.

The Allied commanders on the Western Front, **General Joffre** and **Sir Douglas Haig**, still believed they could break through the German lines. They agreed that together they would make their biggest attack yet – on the area around the River Somme in France. Thinking that they had plenty of time to prepare the attack, they began to train and equip 105,000 men for an advance on both sides of the river.

But General Falkenhayn also had a plan, and he put his into operation first. Falkenhayn believed he could win the war by focussing his attacks on one small area of the Western Front. The place he chose was the city of Verdun where a great French fortress stood. The fortress of Verdun was a symbol of France's strength, and Falkenhayn knew that the French would defend it to the last drop of their blood. He aimed, as he put it, to 'bleed France white' at Verdun.

The story of 1916 is very much the story of these two plans. For France was indeed 'bled white' at Verdun while, on the Somme, Britain lost almost a whole generation of men in one of the worst slaughters of history.

Britain lost something else in 1916. For over a hundred years her Navy had been the most powerful in the world. But after the battle of Jutland, the only great sea battle of the war, the Royal Navy lost its supremacy. Britannia no longer 'ruled the waves'.

8

VERDUN AND THE SOMME

A still from a film made some weeks later in Britain shows how British soldiers went 'over the top' on the first day of the Battle of the Somme

The Battle of Verdun

The city of Verdun was ringed by thirteen massive concrete forts dug deep into the ground. For many years these forts had made Verdun the strongest city in France, but in 1916 they were useless. Six months earlier the guns had been taken out of the forts to help the armies in other places. Most French people did not know this, however, and they still thought of Verdun as the symbol of their country's strength.

Early in February 1916 the Germans brought 1400 big guns to the hills around the city and at dawn on 21 February they opened fire. Throughout the day two million shells blasted into the forts and then the Germans attacked the trench lines in front of them. They captured the first line after just two days and the second line on the day after. Verdun was about to fall.

At this point, a furious argument broke out between the French generals and the politicians. The generals knew that Verdun was of no military use and were all for giving it up to the Germans. The argument is described by a British historian, A.J.P. Taylor:

'Joffre refused to take the attack seriously . . . he would not allow it to interfere with the preparations for his own attack on the Somme later. Briand, the French Prime Minister, was

less calm. On 24 February Briand motored to Chantilly. Joffre was already in bed asleep. Briand insisted on his being pulled out of bed – for the only time in the war. Officers tried to explain that Verdun was of no importance; indeed they would be glad to get rid of it. Briand lost his temper. He shouted: "You may not think losing Verdun a defeat, but everyone else will. If you surrender Verdun you will be cowards, cowards, and I'll sack the lot of you." Joffre, still apparently half asleep, let the storm blow. Then, opening his eyes, he said softly: "The Prime Minister is right. I agree with him. No retreat at Verdun. We fight to the end."'

General Philippe Pétain was given the job of saving Verdun. He said 'Ils ne passeront pas' – 'They shall not pass'. These simple words inspired the French defenders throughout the battle which followed.

The main problem facing Pétain was a lack of supplies. Men, food and ammunition were urgently needed but only one road into Verdun was still open. A French writer, Paul Heuzé, takes up the story:

'Our High Command's first decision was to prohibit horse-drawn carriages over the whole of this vital road. . . . Without his elementary measure, Verdun would have been lost as the passage of horses would have choked up the whole movement of supplies.

Check points along the road have established that it was used by as many as 6000 vehicles a day, that is, an average of one every fourteen seconds! At one time vehicles even passed at the rate of one every five seconds, and this for hours in a row.'

For five whole months, the convoys of lorries trundled along this road which the French called the **'Sacred Way'**. They poured countless men and supplies into the city and it was this that saved Verdun. Whether it was worth saving is a matter of opinion, for the cost was great. By the time the Germans called off their attack in July, their big guns had fired 23 million shells, killing 315,000 French soldiers and destroying the entire city. The Germans had lost 282,000 men and had failed to break the Western Front.

The Battle of the Somme

While the French and Germans massacred each other at Verdun, a huge British army and a number of French divisions began their offensive along the River Somme. The **Battle of the Somme** started with a five-day bombardment of the German trenches. It had little effect, however, because the Germans had known for weeks that the attack was coming; their scout planes had seen men and guns moving forward into position. They therefore drew back from the front line and built dug-outs more than 12 metres deep.

On 1 July, thinking that the bombardment had weakened the Germans, General Haig sent thirteen divisions – 200,000 men – over the top. George Coppard, a soldier who survived, looked out at the battlefield next day and what he saw tells us what happened to the men who went over the top:

'Hundreds of dead were strung out like wreckage washed up to a high-water mark. Quite as many died on the enemy wire as on the ground, like fish caught in a net. They hung there in grotesque postures. . . . It was clear that there were no gaps in the wire at the time of the attack. Concentrated machine-gun fire from sufficient guns to command every inch of wire had done its terrible work. The Germans must have been reinforcing the wire for months. It was so dense that daylight could barely be seen through it. . . . How did the planners imagine that Tommies [*British soldiers*] would get through the German wire? Who told them that artillery fire would pound such wire to pieces, making it possible to get through? Any Tommy could have told them that shell fire lifts wire up and drops it down, often in a worse tangle than before.'

On that first day of the Battle of the Somme, 20,000 British soldiers were killed and 35,000 wounded, but this did not make General Haig want to change his methods. He ordered more attacks but the same tragic story was repeated each time. Against the advice of experts who said he did not have enough, he sent fifty tanks into the battle in September. Twenty-nine broke down before they even reached the battlefield and the rest soon got stuck in the mud.

By the end of the battle the British and French had lost 620,000 men and the Germans 450,000. The Allies had advanced only 15 kilometres at the farthest point.

Work section

A. This photograph shows Sir Douglas Haig (second from left) and General Joffre talking to David Lloyd George, Britain's War Minister, during the Battle of the Somme. Which of the following statements do you think each man was making?

'I doubt whether we can break through the German lines. They have too many machine-guns and too much barbed wire.'

'What we need is more guns and more shells. With a big enough bombardment and enough men, we can break through the German lines.'

'We are beating the Germans at Verdun. We can do the same here.'

B. In the light of what you have read about the battle of Verdun, do you think the battle was worth fighting? Explain your answer.

C. According to George Coppard, what was the main reason why so many British were killed on the first day of the Battle of the Somme? What other reasons can you suggest?

9

THE WAR AT SEA

Unluckily for Scheer, his plan had already been ruined in 1914 when a drowned German sailor was washed up onto a Russian beach. In his pocket was a book containing all Germany's radio codes. The Russians gave the book to their British allies who were then able to de-code German radio messages. So when they heard Scheer giving coded radio orders to his ships in May 1916, they were able to make plans of their own.

Scheer sent his bait out to sea on 31 May. It was a squadron of ships led by **Admiral Hipper**. Scheer himself put to sea an hour and a half later. Using their captured radio code book, the British picked up his radio messages and sent out the Grand Fleet to meet him.

Never before had two such mighty fleets sailed into battle. Two hundred and fifty great ships were steaming at speed into the misty North Sea.

An Advance Force of British ships led by **Admiral Beatty** went out ahead of the Grand Fleet to meet Hipper's 'bait' squadron. They closed in on each other at a combined speed of 90 kilometres per hour. Hipper's ships quickly sank two of Beatty's cruisers and then chased the rest northwards. Hipper did not realise that he was heading straight for the Grand Fleet.

Just before six in the evening the two great battle fleets came into contact off the coast of Jutland in Denmark. Fierce fighting went on all evening. High explosive shells ripped thick armour plating open as if it was tin. Sailors burned to death or drowned as their ships were hit. Survivors gasped in an icy sea coated

The Battle of Jutland

Before 1916 there were no major sea battles between Britain and Germany, the world's two great naval powers. They had fought minor battles in 1914 at Coronel and the Falkland Islands (see page 7), but since then both sides had been very cautious and kept their distance. The **British Grand Fleet** kept to the safety of Scapa Flow in the Orkney Islands while the **German High Seas Fleet** stayed at anchor in the ports of Kiel, Cuxhaven and Wilhelmshaven.

In January 1916, however, there was a change in Germany's naval command. **Admiral von Scheer** was put in charge of the High Seas Fleet and he was eager for action. His plan was to send a small number of his ships into the North Sea to act as bait for Britain's Grand Fleet. He would then follow, 80 kilometres behind, with the High Seas Fleet to act as the trap when the British took the bait.

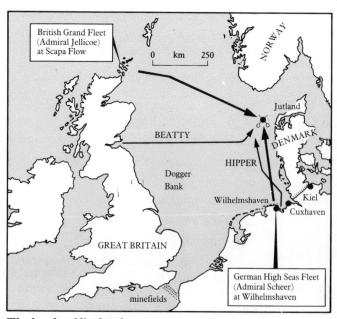

The battle of Jutland

with dirty oil. Then, as darkness fell, Sheer's fleet turned away and headed for home.

Admiral Jellicoe, commander of the British Grand Fleet, did not try to chase Scheer for he feared that German submarines and mines were close by. He too turned around and made his way home. By daybreak the seas off Jutland were empty and the battle was over.

Who won the Battle of Jutland? If you look at the figures below it appears that the German High Seas Fleet was the victor.

Total losses at the Battle of Jutland

	Britain	Germany
Battleships	0	1
Battle cruisers	3	1
Cruisers	3	4
Destroyers	8	5
Men	6077	2551

But the British denied that they had lost the battle. It was, they said, Scheer who gave up first and fled for home. Later in the war they were also able to point out that the German High Seas Fleet stayed at home for the rest of the war, not wanting to risk another great battle.

As you know, judgement about who won the battle is a matter of opinion and it is up to you to make up your own mind on the basis of what you have read.

War under the sea

Beneath the waves, a different sort of battle was taking place between German submarines, or U-boats, and Allied ships. This underwater war began in February 1915 when the Germans announced that the seas around Britain were a 'war zone' in which they would sink any ship without warning. Their aim was to starve Britain into surrender by sinking the supply ships bringing food and weapons to her.

The most famous sinking of a ship in British waters came two months later on 7 May 1915. The British liner *Lusitania* was sailing from New York to Liverpool. Before it set sail, Germany gave a public warning that the liner was likely to be sunk as she was

A torpedo from a U-boat sinks a merchant ship

carrying arms to Britain. Thirteen kilometres off the coast of Ireland Captain Schweiger, of Germany's U-boat 20, spotted the *Lusitania* through his periscope and fired two torpedoes at her. The liner sank in eighteen minutes, taking 1098 of her 1906 passengers and crew to the bottom of the sea.

Submarine attacks on Allied ships continued in 1916. In March, for example, the cross-channel ferry *Sussex* was torpedoed in the English Channel. By the end of the year U-boats had sunk 2,371,000 tonnes of merchant shipping.

To combat the menace of the U-boat the British tried using underwater mines and nets. Mines, anchored to the sea-bed so that they floated beneath the waves, exploded on contact with the hulls of ships or submarines. Huge minefields were laid in the English Channel as well as in the approaches to Germany's ports. The Germans, of course, did all they could to destroy the minefields. As the British minelayers put down the mines, German minesweepers were sent out to cut the cables. A stalemate seemed to be developing at sea, just as it had on the Western Front.

Work section

A. Look back at what you have read about the Battle of Jutland.
1. Why do you think that the British and the Germans both claimed they had won the battle?
2. Which of the two fleets, in your opinion, was the victor?

B. After the Battle of Jutland a British newspaper wrote: 'The German fleet has assaulted its jailor but it is still in jail'. Explain in your own words what you think this means.

C. Why do you think that the Germans decided to sink *all* ships that their U-boats found in British waters?

D. The painting on the opposite page shows one of the sailors who fought in the Battle of Jutland. He was a sixteen-year-old 'Boy First Class' named John Cornwell. He died of injuries two days after the battle and was later awarded the Victoria Cross for gallantry. Find out what John Cornwell did to earn the VC.

10
THE HOME FRONTS

Most people in Europe were enthusiastic about the war when the fighting began. While men rushed off to join the army, the civilians who stayed at home were infected by war fever. Crowds in every country waved flags, sang patriotic songs, gave money for the war effort, and eagerly read every every detail about the battles in their newspapers. By the end of 1916, however, civilians were losing their enthusiasm, for the war was changing their lives in ways they had never expected. Let us see what happened to the civilians in Britain.

War restrictions

The war reduced everybody's freedom. **The Defence of the Realm Act** (or **DORA** as people called it) allowed the government to do almost anything it wanted. It could take away a person's land or censor the newspapers, it could arrest 'troublemakers' or buy goods at rock bottom prices. People hated some of the restrictions that DORA put on them. For example, pubs had to close in the afternoons, the beer was watered down and customers were not allowed to buy rounds of drinks, because the government believed that workers were taking too many of their meal breaks in pubs. DORA was even used to change time. In 1916, everybody had to put their clocks forward one hour so that there would be more daylight during working hours.

Conscription was another way in which people lost some of their freedom. **The Military Service Acts** of 1916 stated that all men between the ages of 18 and 51 had to serve in the armed forces. The people who hated this most were **conscientious objectors** (**COs**) – people who believe that fighting is wrong, for whatever reason. These 'Conshies' or 'Cuthberts', as they were nicknamed, had to go before special tribunals, or courts, to ask to be excused from military service. The courts turned down most of their requests as they thought that being 'soft' on the COs would encourage other men to refuse to fight. Anyway, most people thought the COs were just cowards.

In fact, thousands of COs did heroic war work that did not involve fighting. Many Quakers served as ambulance men in the front lines and won medals for their bravery there.

Food shortages

It was not only restrictions on their freedom that changed the lives of civilians. They were also affected by food shortages. As you have found out, Britain and Germany were trying to starve each other into surrender by sinking each other's supply ships. By 1916, British housewives were having to queue at shops, prepare meatless dishes and use less food in their cooking. In Germany the hunger was far worse. The harvest there had been bad and the winter was bitterly cold. For millions of Germans the only food available was turnips. Thousands of them died during the terrible 'turnip winter' of 1916.

The price of war

Many civilians had their lives changed by the deaths of their loved ones in the fighting. During the four years of the Great War an average of 1500 men were killed every day. After great battles, whole pages of the newspapers were filled with the names of the dead. Every morning, families opened the newspapers in anxiety, praying that the name of a husband or brother or son would not be there in the lists. This naturally made many people less enthusiastic about the war.

Some civilians were finding by 1916 that they themselves risked being killed in the fighting, even though they were far from the battlefields. People on Britain's North Sea coast were killed by shells from German warships in 1914 and 1915, while London was bombed by *Zeppelin* airships and later by *Gotha*

German women scavenging for food scraps

aeroplanes. In all, 1117 people lost their lives in German air raids on Britain.

Women at war

One of the biggest changes that the Great War made to civilian life was in the number of women who went out to work. So many men were needed for the fighting that there were not enough left to work in the factories. At first women worked mainly in the munitions factories, doing the dangerous job of making shells and explosives. Not only did they face the constant risk of accidental explosion, but also damage to their health. The acid fumes in high explosives harmed their lungs and turned their skins bright yellow.

From 1916 onwards, women also began to work on buses and trams, in the police force, delivering coal, ploughing fields, making machinery, nursing, and so on. Before the war most women workers were in domestic service, earning low wages for long hours as maids or cooks. Their new jobs gave them better pay, and that meant more freedom to dress and behave in the way they chose.

More important, before the war was over, women over the age of thirty were given the right to vote. It was the first step towards gaining equal rights with men.

Women at work loading sacks of coke at the South Metropolitan Gas Works in London

Work section

A. This is a list of some of the things that DORA forbade British people to do. Choose four of them and explain why you think these restrictions were introduced.
   1. Talk about naval or military matters in public places.
   2. Spread rumours about military affairs.
   3. Trespass on railways or bridges.
   4. Use code when writing letters abroad.
   5. Light bonfires or fireworks.
   6. Fly kites.
   7. Buy binoculars.
   8. Melt down gold or silver.
   9. Feed bread to dogs, poultry, horses.
   10. Ring church bells.

B. Study this poster which appeared in early 1916.
   1. What was the Military Service Act, 1916?
   2. Explain the meaning of the terms Local Tribunal and Certificate of Exemption.
   3. a) What are your opinions of Conscientious Objectors?
      b) How would you have treated young men who refused to fight?

> ## MILITARY SERVICE ACT, 1916
> Every man to whom the Act applies will on Thursday, March 2nd, be deemed to have enlisted for the period of the War unless he is excepted or exempt.
> ### Any man who has adequate grounds for applying to a Local Tribunal for a
> ## CERTIFICATE OF EXEMPTION UNDER THIS ACT
> ### Must do so BEFORE
> ## THURSDAY, MARCH 2
> Why wait for the Act to apply to you?
> Come **now** and join of your own free will. You can at once put your claim before a Local Tribunal for exemption from being called up for Military Service if you wish.
> ## ATTEST NOW

C. Study the photograph of women working in a coke depot.
   1. What kind of work might they have been doing before the war?
   2. What advantages might there be in this kind of work that women did not have in pre-war jobs?

D. Make notes on *The Events of 1916* before going any farther. You can copy the revision guide on the next page or, if you prefer, use it as a framework for notes of your own.

Revision guide: the events of 1916

A. Both sides believed thay could make a breakthrough on the Western Front in 1916. **Joffre** and **Haig**, the Allied commanders, planned an all-out attack along the River Somme while Germany's commander **Falkenhayn** planned to 'bleed France white' at Verdun by concentrating all his forces there.

B. The Battle of Verdun

1. The fortress city of Verdun had no military value because its guns had been taken away, but it was still a symbol of French strength and pride. General Joffre therefore decided to defend it, whatever the cost.

2. **General Pétain** was given the job of saving Verdun. His motto was 'They shall not pass'. He organised the defence of Verdun by bringing hundreds of thousands of soldiers and supplies along the '**Sacred Way**'.

3. After five months of terrible fighting the Germans gave up their attack. Pétain had saved Verdun, but only at the cost of 315,000 soldiers dead.

C. The Battle of the Somme

1. 200,000 British and French soldiers attacked the German trenches around the River Somme on 1 July 1916. 20,000 British soldiers were killed on the first day alone.

2. More attacks were made during the summer and autumn. **Tanks** were used for the first time in September. But the German line did not break.

3. By the end of the battle over one million men were dead – 620,000 British and French, 450,000 German.

D. The war at sea

1. The **Battle of Jutland** was the only major sea battle between the British and German fleets. Admiral von Scheer tried to trap the British Grand Fleet by sending out a small number of his ships into the North Sea to act as 'bait'. Although the British knew it was a trap they were soundly beaten in the battle that took place off Denmark's coast. Even so, the British claimed victory because it was the German fleet that stopped fighting first, and because the German fleet stayed in port for the rest of the war.

2. **Submarine warfare** was an important part of the war at sea. German U-boats tried to starve Britain into surrender by sinking supply ships with torpedoes. The most famous sinking had already taken place in 1915, when the liner *Lusitania* was sunk. The British tried to combat the U-boats with underwater mines and nets, but without much success.

E. The home front

Civilians in every country were badly affected by the war:

1. **Loss of freedom**: in Britain the **Defence of the Realm Act** allowed the government to do almost anything it liked. The Military Service Acts introduced **conscription** for men between 18 and 51. This led to the problem of what to do with **conscientious objectors**.

2. **Food shortages**: food supplies were disrupted by the war at sea. The Germans were affected most badly, and thousands died of starvation during the 'turnip winter' of 1916.

3. **Loss of morale**: Many civilians lost their enthusiasm for the war when relatives were killed in the fighting.

4. **Bombing**: 1117 British civilians were killed in Zeppelin and Gotha attackes on Britain.

The only good development on the home front was that women gained the opportunity to work in new kinds of jobs and, in 1918, to vote.

PART FOUR

FOUR

NINETEEN SEVENTEEN

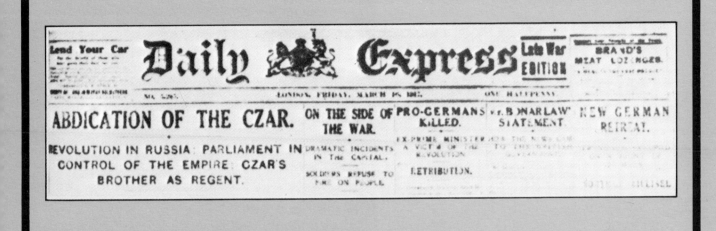

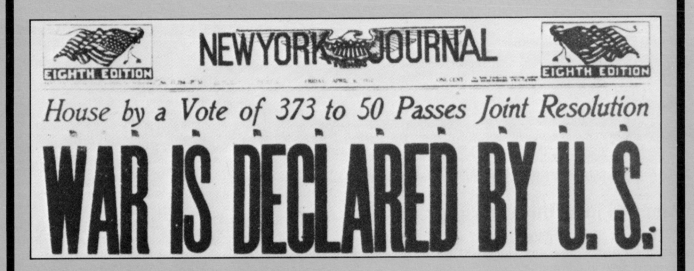

Two newspaper headlines that sum up the key events of 1917

1917 was a bad year for the Allies. The generals on the Western Front continued to sacrifice whole armies to the barbed wire and the machine guns and the heavy artillery – without success. In Italy, the Germans and Austrians crushed the Italian army while, at sea, the German U-boats came close to starving Britain into defeat by sinking her supply ships.

December 1917 brought the worst disaster. Russia had exploded into revolution at the start of the year and after eight months of chaos, a new government surrendered to the Germans. With the Russians out of the war, Germany could now concentrate all its might on the Western Front.

The Allies' only hope of avoiding defeat lay on the other side of the world, in the United States of America. In April the USA declared war on Germany. Within weeks they were sending men and weapons to the Western Front. But could they get enough men to Europe fast enough to stop the Germans? This was the crucial question at the end of 1917, and the year closed without a clear answer.

The only ray of hope for the Allies came from Turkey, Germany's weakest partner in the war. There the Allies scored their only real victories big enough to knock Turkey out of the fighting entirely.

11

THE AMERICANS COME IN, THE RUSSIANS GO OUT

The Russians leave – or try to. A loyal soldier forces deserters to go back to the front line

America joins the war

On 6 April 1917 Britain, France and Russia were joined by a new ally: the United States of America declared war on Germany.

The British people thought the Americans should have joined the war long ago. After all, they spoke the same language and had much in common. The Americans thought differently. To them, the war in Europe was a distant quarrel they had not helped to make and which had nothing to do with them. Their President, Woodrow Wilson, therefore kept America neutral.

But America could not really cut herself off from Europe. Her businessmen were making huge profits from selling weapons to the Allies, and the American government was lending them money. By 1917 these **war loans** amounted to two billion dollars. So while Woodrow Wilson said that America was neutral, he was already involved financially with the Allies.

It was not only money that drew America onto the side of the Allies. Her ships in the Atlantic Ocean were being attacked and sunk by German U-boats. Americans had already suffered when the liner *Lusitania* was torpedoed in 1915, killing 128 of the American passengers on board (see page 23). Anti-German feeling swept through the country and many people demanded that America should go to war with Germany.

After the *Lusitania* sinking, the Germans cut back their U-boat attacks for over a year, but by 1917 they were desperate for a quick victory. They could only do this by starving Britain and France of supplies. So the U-boats were sent out again with orders to attack ships of any nationality sailing in British waters. This was called **unrestricted submarine warfare**. Within eight weeks they had sunk eight American ships. America made strong protests but the U-boats continued their unrestricted submarine warfare.

America's patience finally ran out when news of the **Zimmerman Telegram** was printed in the newspapers. Arthur Zimmerman, Germany's foreign minister, sent a telegram to one of his agents in Mexico, suggesting that Mexico should make an alliance with Germany if America joined the war. The Mexicans could then attack America's southern states such as Texas and Arizona. This was the last straw. President Woodrow Wilson had no choice but to go to war.

America's entry into the war was a great boost to the Allies for she was one of the richest countries in the world. But there was a problem. The Americans could not join the fighting at once. Their army was small and needed to be built up. Weapons had to be made, men trained, and ships built to take them across the Atlantic. This would all take many months.

The Germans now began a race against time to win the war before the Americans arrived.

Revolution in Russia

The chances of Germany winning a quick victory soon began to look good, for the war on the Eastern Front was nearly over. Russia was in revolution and her armies close to collapse. With Russia out of the war, the Germans would be able to concentrate all their forces on the Western Front for a massive new attack.

Revolution had already begun in Russia before America joined the war. The people disliked the rule of their Tsar, Nicholas II, and his German wife, Alexandra. They hated the strange monk, Rasputin, who was the royal couple's closest adviser. They were sick of the war that had already cost millions of Russian lives. They were suffering from food and fuel shortages, and by 1917 they had suffered enough.

Revolution in Russia: a crowd in Petrograd scatters to escape bullets, July 1917

Rioting and strikes began in February and Tsar Nicholas was overthrown. A new **Provisional Government** was set up to rule Russia in his place.

The Provisional Government did little better than Tsar Nicholas. It ordered a new attack on Germany in July and, for a few days, the Russians were victorious. Then the Germans counter-attacked. This was the end of the Russian army. Whole regiments left the battlefields and set off for home. Thousands deserted. In this state of chaos, Communist revolutionaries led by **Vladimir Lenin** staged a second revolution and overthrew the Provisional Government. Only days after coming to power, Lenin announced that Russia would make peace with Germany.

Within the space of seven months, the Allies had gained a powerful new partner and had lost an old one.

Work section

A. This cartoon shows Uncle Sam, the symbol of America, carrying two different messages on the same sandwich board. The cartoon was drawn in 1916 while America was still neutral. Write a few sentences explaining what point you think the cartoonist was trying to make.

B. Before declaring war on Germany, President Woodrow Wilson said this in a speech to Congress (the parliament of the USA):

> 'I advise that the Congress declare the recent course of the Imperial German Government to be in fact nothing less than war against the Government and the People of the United States. . .'

Which of the actions of the German government do you think Wilson had in mind when he made this speech? Explain your answer.

C. 1. Why did Russia make peace with Germany in December 1917?
2. What effect did this have on the Allied war effort?

29

12

MUTINY AND MUD –
THE WESTERN FRONT IN 1917

While America got ready to fight and while Russia seethed with revolution, the generals on the Western Front looked for new ways to break the stalemate of trench warfare.

The Nivelle offensive

The French had a new commander, **General Nivelle**, and he believed he had the answer. Nivelle would find the weakest spot in the German trench line and would smash it with a massive attack. The French armies would then pour through the gap and chase the Germans out of France.

Unfortunately for Nivelle, the Germans knew what was coming. Two weeks before the attack was due to start, they captured a French officer who had the plans in his pockets. They lost no time in preparing for Nivelle's great offensive; they simply retreated to a new line of trenches they had been building for months – the **Hindenburg Line**.

On 9 April the British attacked the town of Arras to draw attention away from Nivelle's offensive. At first it was a success. Canadian troops captured **Vimy Ridge** but then the Germans brought up reserve troops. In the battle that followed there were a quarter of a million casualties.

Farther south, Nivelle began his great offensive but the promised breakthrough never came. The French soldiers rushed at the German trenches only to find them empty. Then moving forward into what they thought was undefended land, they were caught in a trap. Machine-gun fire from all sides mowed them down and destroyed their advance. But Nivelle would not accept defeat and sent more men forward. After ten days of killing, 34,000 of them were dead and another 90,000 were wounded.

Mutiny

General Nivelle had promised his men victory but had failed, and now they turned against him. A mutiny began in the French army. Thousands deserted and set off for home. Fifty-four divisions – half the entire army – refused to obey orders. Discipline collapsed.

In this desperate situation, Nivelle was sacked and replaced by General Pétain, the hero who had saved Verdun. Pétain used ruthless methods to restore discipline. Many thousands of soldiers were court-martialled and hundreds sentenced to death. Some were sent to prison on Devil's Island. Gradually, Pétain gained control of his men. And to improve their morale, he doubled their leave and improved their food rations.

The price to be paid for mutiny. A French soldier about to be shot by his own side, April 1917.

British victories

To draw attention away from the French army mutiny, the British attacked again in the north. Their target was a hill, 140 metres high, at **Messines**. From this hill the Germans could see everything for miles around.

In great secrecy, British engineers dug nineteen tunnels deep under the hill and packed them with half a million kilograms of TNT. On 7 June they were detonated all at once. The explosion, which rattled windows as far away as London, wiped the hill from

Part of the Hindenburg line, also known as the Siegfried Line. Compare it to the picture of trenches on page 13. What advantages did the Germans now have?

the face of the earth and the British were able to advance.

General Haig was so pleased by this success at Messines that he ordered the army to advance to the old battlefield of Ypres. Although it was summer, the weather was the wettest for many years and the Third Battle of Ypres, better known as **Passchendaele**, was the most horrible of the war. Haig started the battle with a bombardment of 4,500,000 shells. This churned the soaking ground into a sea of liquid mud. When the soldiers advanced, even strong men could hardly move as they sank up to their waists. They put down duckboards to cross the mud but tired men or the wounded easily slipped off and drowned in shell holes filled with slime. As the corpses of men and horses rotted beneath the mud the battlefield began to stink – the generals in their headquarters could smell decaying flesh from 8 kilometres away. The oozing ground turned poisonous and mud on a wound usually made it gangrenous.

Four hundred thousand British were killed or wounded in the hell of Passchendaele and by the end of the battle they had won only 800 metres of mud. When General Haig sent one of his officers to visit the battlefield, the officer burst into tears and said 'My God, did we really send men to fight in that?'

Haig now tried a new method of attack. In November he sent 381 tanks towards the German trenches at **Cambrai**. At first it seemed that tanks would be the key to victory for they smashed a gap 8 kilometres wide in the German lines. Ten thousand Germans were taken prisoner and London's church bells rang out in triumph. But the tanks had gone too far, too fast. The soldiers following behind could not keep up with them. The Germans counter-attacked and quickly regained all their lost ground.

Work section

A. These two photographs show the village of Passchendaele from the air before and after the Third Battle of Ypres. Explain in as much detail as you can what happened in the interval between the taking of the two photographs.

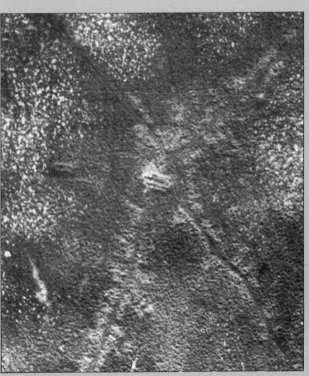

B. Read this account of General Nivelle's offensive, written in 1962, then answer the questions beneath.

'On April 16th, 1917, the French infantry – exhilarated [*excited*] by all they had been promised – left their trenches with an elan unsurpassed in all their glorious history. They advanced half a mile into a vacuum, and then came up against thousands of . . . machine-guns. Angry, demoralised, bitterly disillusioned men flooded back from the scene of the butchery. By the following day there had been something like 120,000 casualties. Nivelle had predicted 10,000 wounded . . . he had broken the French army.'

1. What had the French army been promised, and why were they excited by it?
2. According to the writer, the French 'advanced half a mile into a vacuum'. Explain why there were no German soldiers in the area they attacked.
3. For what reasons can it be said that Nivelle 'had broken the French army'? Do you think this is a fair judgement?

FIGHTS AT SEA, IN THE MOUNTAINS AND THE DESERT

War against the U-boats

Early in 1917 the Germans almost won the war with the use of their U-boats. In April alone they sank nearly one million tonnes of merchant shipping. One out of every four boats leaving Britain's ports never returned. By the end of April only six weeks' supply of food was left in the country. Lord Jellicoe, Britain's naval chief said 'It is impossible for us to go on with the war if losses like this continue'.

The situation was saved by Britain's new Prime Minister, David Lloyd George, who introduced the **convoy system**. The idea was that merchant ships should sail together in large groups, protected by the Royal Navy's destroyers. The system was started in May and had an immediate effect. From then on, only one in a hundred ships leaving British ports were sunk by U-boats. The convoy system had saved Britain from starvation.

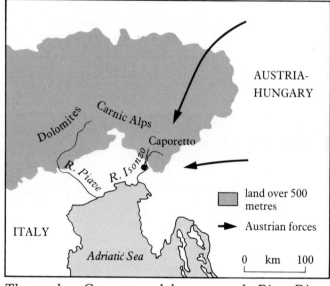

The attack on Caporetto and the retreat to the Piave River

were swept aside in the mad rush. In ten days, the Italians retreated over 100 kilometres to the River Piave. Three hundred thousand men who did not run fast enough were taken prisoner by the Germans, along with 2500 guns and large stocks of food.

The **Battle of Caporetto** was a great victory for the Central Powers and a disaster for the Allies. Italy had come close to being knocked out of the war, and only prompt help from Britain and France stopped this from happening. For months after, they stayed on the Piave, doing no more than defend themselves while they recovered their strength and rebuilt their shattered armies.

A U-boat attacks a merchant ship

Disaster in Italy

Since joining the Allies in 1915 the Italian army had been fighting in one of the most difficult battle areas of Europe – the Alps. Their front was on the Isonzo river where they had fought eleven bloody battles but had never advanced more than 15 kilometres. Now in 1917 the Italian soldiers were worn out by their attempts to break through the icy mountain passes into Austria.

In October the Germans decided it was time to drive the Italians out of the Alps, and sent seven divisions to help their Austrian ally to do this. Together they marched towards the town of **Caporetto**. The Italians were totally unprepared for the attack. Almost the entire army threw down its weapons and fled in panic. Some loyal soldiers tried to stop the retreat by shooting deserters as they crossed bridges, but they

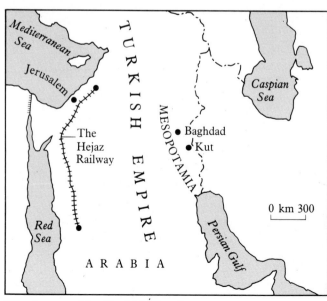

The deserts of the Turkish Empire

The war in the desert

The only gleam of hope for the Allies in 1917 came from the deserts of the Turkish Empire.

British and Indian troops had been fighting the Turks in **Mesopotamia** since 1915. The campaign in 'Mespot', as the soldiers called it, ended in defeat when the Turks surrounded them at **Kut** and forced them to surrender after a long siege. However, the Turks then withdrew many of their troops to fight in other places, and this gave a new British force the chance to fight back. In March 1917 they captured the ancient city of Baghdad and went on to take control of the rest of 'Mespot'.

In another part of the Turkish Empire, Arabia, the British had even more success against the Turks. The Arabs had risen in revolt against their Turkish rulers a year before, and the British sent a number of officers to Arabia to find out what was going on there. One of them, Colonel T.E. Lawrence, quickly became a friend of Emir Feisal, son of the Arab leader.

Before long, '**Lawrence of Arabia**' was helping the Arabs to organise themselves into guerilla groups. The tough Arab tribesmen were impressed by the small, fair-haired Englishman who spoke their language, dressed like them, rode camels expertly, and who loved the desert. They gave him their trust and followed him in attacks on Turkish strongholds and on the Hejaz Railway, an important supply route across the desert. These attacks tied down large numbers of Turks who were sent to guard the railway.

While this guerilla war was going on, one of Britain's best generals, **Sir Edmund Allenby**, led an army of British and Australian troops into another part of the Turkish Empire – Palestine. At the Battle of Beersheba he forced the Turks to retreat and in December captured the holy city of Jerusalem.

Work section

A. Study this poster put out by the British government in 1917. Explain as fully as you can what the government was trying to achieve with this sort of poster. Try to deal with the following points in your explanation:

1. The effects of U-boat attacks on Britain's food supplies.
2. Why it was important for British people to 'eat less bread'.

B. Read this extract from a book written by 'Lawrence of Arabia', then answer the questions beneath.

'Round the bend, whistling its loudest, came the train, a splendid two-engined thing of twelve passenger coaches, travelling at top speed . . . .I touched off a mine under the first driving wheel of the first locomotive, and the explosion was terrific . . . . The train was badly derailed, with the listing coaches butted end to end at all angles, zigzagged across the track. One of them was a saloon decorated with flags. In it had been Mehmed Jemal Pasha, commanding the 8th Army Corps, hurrying down to defend Jerusalem.'

1. What was the name of the railway described here? What was its importance?
2. What was Lawrence's aim in blowing up trains travelling on this railway?
3. Why do you think the Turkish army commander was 'hurrying down' to Jerusalem?

C. Make notes on *The Events of 1917* before going any further. You can copy the revision guide on the next page or, if you prefer, use it as a framework for notes of your own. Illustrate your notes with maps.

Revision Guide: The events of 1917

A. Two important changes took place among the Allies

    1. The **USA declared war** on Germany in April because

        a) German U-boats were sinking American ships;

        b) The **Zimmermann Telegram** suggested that Germany would help Mexico to attack the southern states of America.

    2. **Russia made peace with Germany** in December because

        a) The Russian armies had collapsed after a major defeat in July;

        b) A new, Communist government came to power in a revolution (November), and one of its main aims was to give peace to the war-weary Russian people.

B. Events on the Western Front

    1. The **Nivelle Offensive** (April) promised a quick victory for the Allies but it failed because the Germans drew back to a new line of strongly defended trenches, the **Hindenburg Line**.

    2. The **French army mutinied** after this defeat. Nivelle was sacked and a new commander, General Pétain, restored order by using ruthless punishments and by improving soldiers' conditions.

    3. The British won minor successes in battles at **Vimy ridge** (April) and **Messines** (June) and were able to move forward. But in the Third Battle of Ypres, or **Passchendaele**, they fought in the worst conditions of the entire war, suffering 400,000 casualties and winning only 800 metres of land. In November, a massed tank attack at **Cambrai** broke the German lines for a while but a German counter-attack soon reversed this victory.

C. Unrestricted submarine warfare almost knocked Britain out of the war in April. German U-boats were sinking a quarter of all supply ships and there was only six weeks food supply left in the country. The situation was saved by using the **convoy system** for merchant ships.

D. Italy was almost knocked out of the war at the **Battle of Caporetto** (October). The Italian army had to abandon the Isonzo Front and retreated in panic to the River Piave.

E. The war in Turkey brought the only Allied successes of 1917.

    1. The British captured Baghdad in March and went on to take control of the rest of **Mesopotamia**.

    2. Arab attacks on the Hejaz Railway, led by '**Lawrence of Arabia**', cut off Turkish supplies and tied down large numbers of Turkish soldiers sent to guard the railway.

    3. **General Allenby** defeated a Turkish army at Beersheba and then captured the holy city of **Jerusalem** in November.

PART
FIVE
NINETEEN EIGHTEEN

A British cartoon of 1918: Kaiser Wilhelm watches the sands of time run out for his armies

On 3 March 1918 the Germans and Russians signed a peace treaty, the **Treaty of Brest-Litovsk**, ending the war on the Eastern front. The German army which had defeated Russia was now sent to fight on the Western Front. A million soldiers and 3000 big guns arrived there in the spring of 1918, making the German army much stronger than the Allied armies. It began to look as if Germany would win the war.

But time was running out and they knew it. They calculated that they had six months at most before the Americans began flooding into Europe to help the Allies. Then all would be lost.

Germany's **General Ludendorff** decided to gamble everything he had on a final, all-out offensive on the Western Front. Two hundred divisions were put under his command for a mighty hammer blow that would break the stalemate and win the war for Germany. He had the men and the weapons necessary for victory – but the question was, did he have enough time?

14
THE LUDENDORFF OFFENSIVE

The German offensive

21 March was the day that General Ludendorff chose for his great offensive. Before dawn, 6000 big guns burst out in a shattering bombardment that lasted five hours. Deadly mustard gas billowed out to blind and suffocate the Allies in their trenches. Then, moving under the cover of dense fog, seventy German divisions dashed forwards towards the British lines. Totally outnumbered and confused, the British climbed out of their trenches and ran. The Germans had broken the stalemate on the Western Front and were now marching through open country towards Paris.

In this crisis, the French and British leaders decided to place all the Allied armies under the command of one general, a Frenchman, **Ferdinand Foch**. His job was to make sure that the British, French and American armies acted as a single force instead of as separate units.

At first it seemed that the Germans were unstoppable and that Foch could do nothing. The Germans advanced 65 kilometres and by July they had reached the River Marne. For the second time in the war it looked as if Paris would fall.

In fact, Ludendorff's gamble had already failed. He

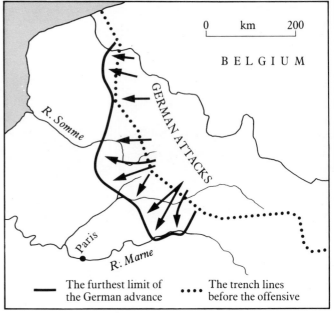

The Ludendorff Offensive

had sent too many men too far, too fast into French territory. Now he had no reserves to send after his exhausted army. Worse still, his rapid advance had made a salient, or bulge, 130 kilometres long and 65

Specially trained German shock troops in gas masks attack French positions through thick woods

kilometres wide. As you can see from the map on the opposite page this meant that his forces could be attacked from three sides.

Meanwhile, Foch had been keeping men in reserve, and American soldiers were arriving in France at the rate of 50,000 a week. On 18 July he gathered all these forces for a great counter-attack. After a fortnight of heavy fighting they drove the Germans back from the Marne. Foch kept up the pressure. On 8 August he sent British forces into the attack, led by 456 tanks. From that day on the Germans retreated continuously until they were back at the Hindenburg Line.

Victory for the Allies

While Ludendorff was gambling away his armies, the Allies were winning victories on other fronts. In Salonika they made a sudden advance against the Bulgarian army and forced it to surrender. In October the Italians crossed the River Piave and won a great victory over the Austrians at the **Battle of Vittorio Veneto**. Turkey was defeated in the same month when General Allenby advanced north from Palestine. And in Germany itself the civilians on the home front were near to collapse. Thousands were dying of starvation while an outbreak of Spanish influenza was killing hundreds every day. Riots were common, talk of revolution was in the air.

Germany could no longer avoid defeat, but Ludendorff hoped at least to delay it. He persuaded the government to write to President Woodrow Wilson of the USA, asking for an **armistice** – an end to the fighting. He knew that Wilson was a moderate man who wanted to offer Germany fair terms of peace. Meanwhile the German army could build up its strength to fight again later.

Revolution in Germany

But while Woodrow Wilson and the Allies talked about whether to offer Germany fair peace terms, a revolution broke out there. In a last attempt to win a victory at sea, the High Seas Fleet was ordered to get up steam and make ready for battle. But the sailors refused to put to sea and began a mutiny. After taking control of their ships they went ashore and took over the town of **Kiel**. Sailors in other ports followed their example and mutiny quickly turned into full-scale revolution.

As the revolution swept through Germany, the army generals took matters into their own hands. They sent two politicians to France to sign an armistice, whatever the terms. Another politician was sent to Kaiser Wilhelm to tell him that the army would no longer take orders from him. That same day, Wilhelm quietly left Germany and fled to Holland, never to return. A **Republic** was set up in place of his empire.

Two days later, Foch met the two German politicians in his personal railway carriage at Compiègne in northern France. When the terms of the armistice were read out, one of them began to cry, for the terms were harsh. But there was no choice but to sign. They put their signatures to the paper at five in the morning of 11 November 1918. Foch left the carriage without shaking their hands. The Great War was over.

Work section

A.   Study this document carefully, noting the date when it was issued.
Then answer these questions.

1. a) Why did 'the enemy' begin 'terrific attacks' against the Allies three weeks before this order was made?
   b) Why were the attacks successful?

2. Do you agree with the statement (line 5) that 'he has as yet made little progress'? Explain your answer.

3. Why do you think Haig gave this order to all soldiers in the British army?

4. Some soldiers were disheartened by this Special Order. Why do you think it had this effect on them?

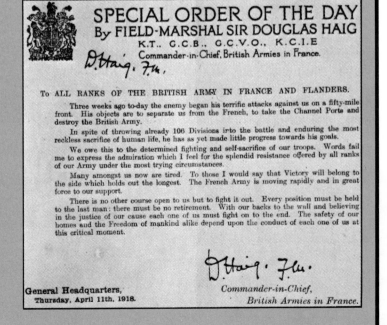

SPECIAL ORDER OF THE DAY
By FIELD-MARSHAL SIR DOUGLAS HAIG
K.T., G.C.B., G.C.V.O., K.C.I.E
D. Haig. 7.4.
Commander-in-Chief, British Armies in France.

To ALL RANKS OF THE BRITISH ARMY IN FRANCE AND FLANDERS.

Three weeks ago to-day the enemy began his terrific attacks against us on a fifty-mile front. His objects are to separate us from the French, to take the Channel Ports and destroy the British Army.

In spite of throwing already 106 Divisions into the battle and enduring the most reckless sacrifice of human life, he has as yet made little progress towards his goals.

We owe this to the determined fighting and self-sacrifice of our troops. Words fail me to express the admiration which I feel for the splendid resistance offered by all ranks of our Army under the most trying circumstances.

Many amongst us now are tired. To those I would say that Victory will belong to the side which holds out the longest. The French Army is moving rapidly and in great force to our support.

There is no other course open to us but to fight it out. Every position must be held to the last man: there must be no retirement. With our backs to the wall and believing in the justice of our cause each one of us must fight on to the end. The safety of our homes and the Freedom of mankind alike depend upon the conduct of each one of us at this critical moment.

D. Haig. 7.4.
Commander-in-Chief,
British Armies in France.

General Headquarters,
Thursday, April 11th, 1918.

B.   List as many reasons as you can why General Ludendorff's great offensive failed.

C.   Study the photograph on the opposite page. What was unusual about this kind of fighting on the Western Front?

D.   Make notes on *The Events of 1918*, using the summary on page 40 to help you.

15
PEACE

The armistice which was signed in Marshal Foch's railway carriage came into effect at 11 o'clock on 11 November 1918. These pictures and words tell the story of how civilians and soldiers reacted to the news that the Great War was over.

London

'. . . with a school friend I took a bus to Woolwich, staying on at the terminus and returning in the same bus to Croydon. From the open upper-deck we watched the crowds singing, shouting, dancing, embracing, vomiting, climbing on the tops of taxis, grabbing one another, and making off into the parks. It was, to me, an eerie and disturbing, rather than a joyful scene – those flushed animal faces, dishevelled women, hoarse voices.' (Written by Malcolm Muggeridge, a British journalist, in his autobiography, *Chronicles of Wasted Time*, 1972).

'Work ceased in shops and offices . . . . Crowds surged through the streets, often led by troops on leave. Omnibuses were seized, and people in strange garments caroused on the upper deck. A bonfire heaped against the plinth of Nelson's column in Trafalgar Square has left its mark to this day. Total strangers copulated [*had sexual intercourse*] in doorways and on the pavements. They were asserting the triumph of life over death. The celebrations ran on with increasing wildness for three days, when the police finally intervened and restored order.' (Written by A.J.P. Taylor, a British historian in his book *English History 1914–1945*, 1965)

The Daily Mirror *announces the end of the war*

Crowds celebrate the end of the war, Paris

On the Western Front

'He would not be killed . . . no one else in the batallion would be killed. . . . Incredible. A thrill of almost painful exultation went through him. . . . Then with a worse, almost unmendable pang, he thought of the millions of men of many nations who would never feel that ecstasy, who were gone for ever, rotting in desolate battlefields and graveyards all over the world. He turned his head farther from the men to hide the tears, which, to his amazement, came into his eyes. Would they dare to maffick [*celebrate wildly*] in London and Paris? Probably. Well let them. Perhaps the men's quietness and lack of demonstration meant that they too felt this.

Ellerton (like them) was indeed quietly and deeply grateful that the long torture was over, but neither he nor they could join with the Captains and the Kings in shouting the victory. The only victory that had resulted was in fact the victory of death over life, of stupidity over intelligence, of hatred over humanity. It must never happen again, never, never.' (Written by David Jones, *In Parenthesis*, 1938)

Work section

A. Read the accounts of Armistice Day in London written by Malcolm Muggeridge and A.J.P. Taylor, then answer these questions:

1. a) Why, according to A.J.P. Taylor, did total strangers copulate in the streets?
   b) In what way does Malcolm Muggeridge's account confirm that some people did this? What different explanation of their behaviour does Malcolm Muggeridge suggest?

2. According to both writers, what other unusual forms of behaviour could be seen in London on Armistice day?

3. Which of the two accounts do you think is the more reliable? Explain your answer.

B. Read the account by David Jones of how soldiers on the Western Front reacted to the news of the Armistice.

1. a) What feelings did the soldiers have when they heard that the war was over?
   b) Why do you think the feelings of the soldiers were so different to those of people in Paris and London?

2. Judging by what you have read in this book, do you agree that the only victory which had been won was 'the victory of death over life, of stupidity over intelligence, of hatred over humanity'? Explain your answer fully.

Revision guide: the events of 1918

A. The Ludendorff Offensive

1. **General Ludendorff** planned to make a final, all-out offensive on the Western Front, hoping to win the war before the Americans could reinforce the Allies. He had more men and more guns than ever before because the end of the war with Russia released German armies from the Eastern Front.

2. The offensive was successful at first. The Germans advanced 65 kilometres, breaking the stalemate of trench warfare, and threatening Paris.

3. To deal with this crisis, **Marshal Foch** was put in sole command of the Allied armies. He counter-attacked in July and steadily drove the Germans back to the Hindenburg Line.

B. The collapse of Germany's allies

1. Bulgaria surrendered after defeat on the Salonika Front.

2. Austria was beaten by the Italians at the **Battle of Vittorio Veneto**.

3. Turkey was beaten by General Allenby's advance from Jerusalem.

C. The German revolution

1. Ludendorff hoped to put off Germany's defeat by asking the Americans for an **armistice** on fair terms, giving his armies time to recover.

2. In November, German sailors at **Kiel** mutinied and started a revolution which swept through the whole country. Kaiser Wilhelm abdicated and Germany became a **republic**.

3. With the country in a state of revolution, the Germans could not go on fighting. They made an unconditional surrender and signed a harsh armistice agreement on 11 November 1918.

Revision quiz

Below is a scrambled set of twenty names and events. Your task is to unscramble them by joining them into pairs and then explaining the connection between them. Do this by dividing a sheet of paper into three columns.

Example:

Conscription	Conscientious objectors	Conscription meant that all men between eighteen and fifty-one had to serve in the armed forces. Some men refused to join the army because they believed that fighting and killing is wrong. Such men were called conscientious objectors.

Verdun.   The Arab Revolt.   Conscription.   Alfred Zimmerman.

'The Old Contemptibles'.   Gallipoli.   U-boats.   The Anzacs.

The mutiny of the French army in 1917.   The 'Sacred Way'.

The Battle of Tannenberg.   The British Expeditionary Force.

Colonel T.E. Lawrence.   Conscientious objectors.   *Lusitania*.

General Nivelle.   The American declaration of war on Germany.

Vladimir Lenin.   General Samsonov.   The Russian revolution.